FINANCIAL PLANNING 101

A Comprehensive Guide to Planning Your Financial Future

CARLA DAVIES

Table of Contents

CHAPTER 1: Introduction to Financial Planning

Financial planning is an essential part of life, but it doesn't have to be complicated. It's important to have a plan in place so that you can make wise decisions about your money and your future. Whether you're just starting out or you've been managing your money for a while, here's a look at financial planning 101.

Start by creating a budget. This is a spending plan that outlines how you're going to allocate your money each month. It should include your income, fixed expenses such as rent, utilities, and loan payments, and discretionary expenses such as entertainment and restaurants. Make sure you're realistic when budgeting and leave a little room for unexpected expenses.

Once you've created a budget, you'll need to start paying down any existing debt. This includes credit cards, student loans, and car loans. It's important to make sure you're making at least the minimum payments on all of your debts each month. If you can, try to pay off the debt with the highest interest rate first.

Next, you'll want to start saving for the future. This includes setting aside money for retirement, college, and other long-term goals. It's important to have a plan for how much you'll be able to save each month and where you'll be investing your money. There are a variety of retirement accounts available, such as a traditional IRA or a Roth IRA. Additionally, many employers offer 401(k)s and other retirement savings plans.

You'll also want to consider establishing an emergency fund. This is a savings account that you can dip into in the event of a job loss, health issue, or other unexpected expense. Aim to save three to six months' worth of living expenses in your emergency fund.

Finally, it's important to stay informed about your finances. Read the news, talk to family and friends, and do your own research on financial topics. Additionally, consider working with a financial advisor or taking a class to further your financial knowledge.

Financial planning is an essential part of life, but it doesn't have to be complicated. Start by creating a budget and then pay down any existing debt. Next, you'll want to start saving for the future, including retirement and other long-term goals. Don't forget to establish an emergency fund and stay informed about your finances. With a little planning, you can be sure that your finances are in order and you're on track to achieve your goals.

What is Financial Planning?

Financial planning is a process that allows individuals and families to make informed decisions about their financial future. It involves creating a budget, setting long-term and short-term goals, and developing strategies to reach those goals. Financial planning is a process that allows you to see the big picture of your financial life and plan for the future.

At its most basic, financial planning is about managing your money. It involves budgeting, saving, investing, and protecting your assets. It includes identifying your financial goals and creating a plan to reach them. Financial planning also involves assessing your financial situation, understanding your risk tolerance, and evaluating your current investments.

Financial planning is important because it helps you make informed decisions about your finances. It can help you save money, invest wisely, and protect your assets. Financial planning can also help you make sure you are able to reach your financial goals.

There are three main steps in financial planning:

1. Set Financial Goals: The first step in financial planning is to identify your financial goals. This should include both long-term and short-term goals. By setting goals, you can create a roadmap for your financial success.

2. Create a Budget: The second step in financial planning is to create a budget. A budget is a plan for how you will allocate your income and expenses. It is important to create a budget that is realistic and reflects your current financial situation.

3. Develop a Strategy: The third step in financial planning is to develop a strategy to reach your financial goals. This should include an investment plan, an emergency fund, and a plan to reduce debt.

Financial planning is not a one-time activity. It is an ongoing process that should be revisited regularly. As your goals, financial situation, and risk tolerance change, your financial plan should be adjusted accordingly.

Financial planning is an important part of your overall financial strategy. It can help you set and reach your financial goals, save money, and make wise investments. By having a financial plan, you can better manage your finances and make informed decisions about your finances.

Benefits of Financial Planning

Financial planning is a vital part of taking control of your finances, and it can mean the difference between having enough money to live comfortably and just getting by. It's important to understand the basics of financial planning so that you can plan for your future and protect yourself from unexpected financial surprises.

When it comes to finances, a little bit of planning can go a long way. Financial planning helps you determine where your money is coming from and where it is going and can help you make better decisions about how to handle your money and reach your goals.

The Benefits of Financial Planning

When it comes to the benefits of financial planning, the most obvious is that it can help you reach your financial goals. By defining your goals and creating a plan to reach them, you are more likely to stick to them and make progress.

Financial planning can also help you save money. By budgeting and tracking your spending, you will be able to identify areas where you are spending too much and make changes that will help you save. In addition, financial planning can help you make wise investments and plan for retirement.

Financial planning can also help you protect your financial future. By understanding the risks and benefits associated with different investments, you can make informed decisions about how to protect your money. This includes creating an emergency fund to help you cover unexpected expenses, creating insurance policies to protect you and your family, and creating a will that ensures your estate is divided according to your wishes.

Finally, financial planning can help you stay organized and on top of your finances. By having a clear plan for your money, you will be able to easily track your progress and make sure you are meeting your goals.

Creating a Financial Plan

Creating a financial plan may seem intimidating, but it doesn't have to be. Start by assessing your current financial situation, including your income, expenses, debts, and assets. Once you have a better understanding of your finances, you can create a budget that outlines how you will allocate your money.

Next, you'll want to set financial goals. These goals should be specific, measurable, attainable, relevant, and time-bound (SMART). For example, you could set a goal of saving a certain amount of money each month or achieving a certain level of debt within a certain time frame.

Once you have defined your goals, you can create an action plan to help you reach them. This should include budgeting, cutting back on expenses, and investing in the right places. You should also consider creating an emergency fund, purchasing insurance, and creating a will.

Finally, you'll want to track your progress and make adjustments as needed. As your situation changes, you will need to adjust your plan to reflect your new reality.

Conclusion

Financial planning is a critical part of taking control of your finances and achieving your goals. By understanding the basics of financial planning and creating a plan to reach your goals, you can save money, protect your financial future, and stay organized. With a little bit of planning, you can ensure a bright financial future for yourself and your family.

CHAPTER 2: Setting Financial Goals

Financial planning is an important part of life. It helps you create a roadmap for spending, saving and investing that meets your needs and goals. Setting financial goals allows you to plan for your future, and is a key part of ensuring your financial security. With the right plan in place, you can ensure that you have the resources to meet your short-term and long-term needs.

Here are some tips for getting started with setting financial goals:

1. Establish Your Priorities

The first step in setting financial goals is to identify your priorities. Ask yourself what matters to you most in life and make sure your financial goals reflect those values. Think about your current and future needs, wants and desires and determine what you want to accomplish financially in order to achieve those objectives.

2. Set Realistic Goals

Once you have established your priorities, it's time to set realistic goals. Make sure your goals are achievable and have a timeline associated with them. For example, if you want to save for a down payment on a house, make sure you have a timeline and a plan for how much you need to save each month in order to reach that goal.

3. Develop a Plan

Once you've identified your priorities and set realistic goals, it's time to develop a plan. Think about what steps you need to take in order to reach your goals. Consider budgeting, increasing your income, reducing expenses, investing, and creating a debt repayment plan.

4. Track Your Progress

Once you've developed a plan, it's important to track your progress. Set up a system that allows you to monitor your progress and make adjustments to your plan if needed. This will help ensure that you are on track to reach your goals.

5. Be Flexible

It's important to remember that your financial goals are not set in stone. Your needs and wants may change over time, so it's important to be flexible and adjust your plan as needed.

Setting financial goals is an important part of ensuring your financial security. It allows you to create a roadmap for spending, saving and investing that meets your needs and goals. By establishing your priorities, setting realistic goals, developing a plan, tracking your progress and being flexible, you can ensure that your financial goals are met.

Planning for the Short-term

Financial planning is a process that helps individuals, families, and businesses make informed decisions about their money and how they will use it to achieve their goals. This planning process typically involves setting financial goals, creating a budget, and determining how to invest and save money to reach these goals. Financial planning is an important part of managing your finances, as it allows you to assess your current situation, identify potential risks and opportunities, and develop strategies to ensure your financial success in the future.

The first step in financial planning is to set short-term goals. Short-term goals are objectives you hope to achieve within the next year or two. These goals should be specific and measurable, and should be based on your current financial situation and future plans. Common short-term goals include saving for a down payment on a house, paying off credit card debt, or saving for a vacation. Setting short-term goals gives you a clear path to follow and helps you stay on track with your financial goals.

Once you've set your short-term goals, you need to create a budget. This budget should be based on the amount of money you earn, your current expenses, and any additional costs associated with your short-term goals. When creating your budget, make sure to include an emergency fund in case of unexpected expenses.

Once you've created your budget, you need to determine how you're going to save and invest to reach your short-term goals. Investing and saving can help you reach your goals faster and can also help you build wealth in the long term. Investing is generally a good idea if you have enough money to invest, as it can provide you with greater returns than saving alone. However, if you don't have enough money to invest or don't feel comfortable investing, then saving is a good option. Consider investing in mutual funds, stocks, bonds, or other types of investments to help you reach your short-term goals.

Once you've created your budget and determined how you're going to save and invest, you need to review your plan periodically. This will help you stay on track with your short-term goals and ensure you're making progress. Additionally, it's important to review your plan in light of any changes in your financial situation. If you experience a change in income, job, or expenses, you should adjust your plan accordingly.

Financial planning is an important part of managing your finances. By setting short-term goals, creating a budget, and determining how to save and invest, you can make informed decisions about your money and ensure you're on track to reach your financial goals.

Planning for the Long-term

Financial planning is a broad term that encompasses a range of activities and strategies designed to ensure one's financial security over the long-term. It can involve planning for the future, budgeting, saving, investing, and even estate planning. For those just starting to think about their financial future, financial planning can seem overwhelming. But with a few simple steps and some guidance, even the most financially inexperienced individual can be on their way to financial security.

The first step in financial planning is to assess your current financial situation. This includes taking an inventory of your assets, liabilities, income, and expenses. Consider your current savings and investments, debt, income sources, and spending habits. This assessment will provide you with a snapshot of your current financial situation and will be the foundation of your financial plan.

Once you have a good understanding of your finances, it is time to set some realistic financial goals. These goals should be specific and measurable, and reflect your priorities. For example, if you want to save for retirement, set a specific target for the amount you want to save and the timeframe in which you want to save it. Or if you want to pay down your student loan debt, set a target for the amount you want to pay off each month.

Once you have set your goals, it is time to create a budget. A budget is a tool that will help you manage your financial resources and reach your goals. A budget should include your income and expenses, as well as any savings and debt repayment goals. When creating your budget, be sure to be realistic. Make sure your expenses don't exceed your income and that you can realistically meet your goals.

Now that you have a budget in place, it is time to start saving and investing. This includes setting up a savings account, investing in stocks and bonds, and using tax-advantaged accounts such as IRAs and 401(k)s. When investing, it is important to keep in mind the importance of diversification. Diversification means investing in different kinds of investments, so that if one type of investment performs poorly, you are still protected by other investments.

Finally, it is important to consider estate planning. This includes creating a will, setting up a trust, and choosing a financial power of attorney. Estate planning helps ensure that your assets are distributed as you wish, and that your family and loved ones are taken care of if something happens to you.

Financial planning is a complex and often daunting process, but it doesn't have to be. With a few simple steps and some guidance, even the most financially inexperienced individual can be on their way to financial security. Start by assessing your current financial situation, setting realistic goals, creating a budget, investing, and considering estate planning. With a little bit of effort, you can be well on your way to financial freedom.

CHAPTER 3: Understanding Your Finances

Do you ever feel overwhelmed when it comes to managing your finances? Don't worry, you're not alone. Many people struggle to make sense of their finances, and it can be a confusing and intimidating process.

The good news is that financial planning doesn't have to be a daunting task. With a few simple steps, you can have a better understanding of your finances and be on your way to achieving your financial goals.

Here's a step-by-step guide to financial planning:

1. Set Financial Goals

The first step to financial planning is to decide what you want to achieve. This could include short-term goals such as paying off credit card debt or building an emergency fund, or long-term goals such as buying a home or retiring early.

Write down your goals and determine the timeline for achieving them. This will give you something to work towards and help you stay motivated.

2. Track Your Spending

Now that you have set financial goals, it's time to take a look at your current spending habits. Do you know how much you're spending each month? Where is your money going?

Tracking your spending is essential to understanding your finances. You can use a spreadsheet, a budgeting app, or simply write it down in a notebook.

3. Create a Budget

Once you have a better understanding of where your money is going, you can create a budget. This will allow you to better manage your money and put yourself in a better position to achieve your financial goals.

Start by listing your essential expenses, such as rent and utilities. Then, list your non-essential expenses such as eating out, entertainment, and shopping.

When creating your budget, set a realistic goal for how much you want to spend in each category. This will help you stick to your budget and make sure you're not overspending.

4. Save for Emergencies

Unexpected expenses can happen at any time, which is why it's important to have an emergency fund. This fund should cover at least three to six months of living expenses in case you encounter a financial emergency.

Start by setting aside a small amount each month, and increase the amount as you can. This will help ensure that you're prepared if you encounter a financial emergency.

5. Invest for the Future

Once you've established an emergency fund, it's time to start investing for the future. Investing is a great way to build wealth, and there are many options to choose from.

Do your research, and speak to a financial advisor if you're unsure where to start. With the right investments, you can achieve your long-term financial goals and build a secure financial future.

6. Monitor Your Progress

Financial planning is an ongoing process. It's important to regularly review your finances and adjust your budget and investments as needed.

This will help you stay on track and ensure that you're making progress towards your goals.

Financial planning doesn't have to be complicated. By taking the time to understand your finances, you can make progress towards achieving your financial goals and build a secure financial future.

Creating a Budget

Creating a budget is one of the most important steps to take when it comes to financial planning. It's often the first step in helping you reach your financial goals and can help you better manage your money. A budget is an essential tool that allows you to track your income and expenses, plan for the future, save money, and more.

Creating a budget can seem daunting, but it doesn't have to be. With a little bit of planning, you can create a budget that works for you and your lifestyle. Here are some tips to help you get started.

1. Establish Your Income

The first step to creating a budget is to figure out how much money you have coming in. This includes all sources of income, such as your salary, investments, side hustles, and more. Make sure to include all sources of income to get an accurate picture of your financial situation.

2. Calculate Your Expenses

The next step is to figure out how much money you're spending each month. This includes all of your fixed expenses, such as rent, utilities, and car payments, as well as variable expenses, such as groceries and entertainment. Make sure to include all of your expenses, even the small ones, so that you get a comprehensive picture of your spending habits.

3. Prioritize Your Expenses

Once you've calculated your income and expenses, it's time to prioritize. This means taking a look at your expenses and deciding which ones are most important and need to be paid first. This could include things like rent, utilities, and car payments, or it could include things like groceries and entertainment. Prioritizing your expenses can help you make sure you're paying for the things that are most important to you.

4. Set Goals and Establish a Savings Plan

Once you have a good idea of your income and expenses, it's time to set some goals. This could include anything from buying a house, to saving for retirement, to paying off debt. After you've set your goals, it's important to create a savings plan to make sure you're on track to reach them. This could include setting up automatic transfers to a savings account or investing in a retirement plan.

5. *Monitor Your Progress*

The final step to creating a budget is to regularly monitor your progress. Make sure to check in on your budget and spending habits every month to make sure you're staying on track. This can help you make sure you're meeting your financial goals and staying within your budget.

Creating a budget is an essential step in financial planning. It can help you better manage your money, set and reach your goals, and save for the future. With a little bit of planning, you can create a budget that works for you and your lifestyle.

Managing Debt

When it comes to financial planning, managing debt should be one of your top priorities. Debt can quickly become overwhelming and can be difficult to manage on your own. As such, it's important to understand the basics of debt and how to properly manage it in order to keep your finances in order.

Debt can come in many forms, including credit cards, student loans, personal loans, car loans, and more. Managing debt can be a difficult task, but it is essential to know how to do it correctly.

First, it's important to understand the different types of debt and how they work. Credit cards, for example, are a type of revolving debt, meaning that you can make purchases up to a certain limit and pay them back over time. Student loans are often a type of installment debt, meaning that you borrow a set amount of money and pay it back over a fixed period of time.

Next, you need to understand the different types of interest rates associated with different types of debt. Interest rates are the fees you are charged for borrowing money, and they can vary from one debt to another. Credit cards have higher interest rates than most other forms of debt, so it's important to pay them off as quickly as possible in order to avoid getting stuck with high interest payments.

Once you understand the different types of debt and their associated interest rates, it's time to create a plan for managing your debt. The first step is to create a budget. This will help you track your income and expenses and give you a better idea of how much you can afford to pay off each month.

Once you know how much you can afford to pay each month, you should start paying off your debts in order of interest rate. Paying off the debts with the highest interest rates first will save you the most money in the long run.

It's also important to be aware of the fees associated with certain types of debt, such as late payment fees or over-the-limit fees. These fees can quickly add up, so it's important to make sure you are staying on top of your payments and avoiding these fees whenever possible.

Finally, if you are having trouble managing your debt on your own, it's important to seek help. There are a number of organizations and services available to help you manage your debt, including credit counseling services and debt consolidation companies. These services can provide you with the guidance you need to get your finances back on track.

Managing debt is an important part of financial planning and can be a difficult task. However, by understanding the different types of debt, the associated interest rates, and creating a plan to pay off your debts, you can ensure that your finances remain in order and that you remain debt free.

CHAPTER 4: Building an Emergency Fund

An emergency fund is a crucial piece of your financial security. It's a savings account that you can draw on in times of financial hardship or unexpected expenses. Without one, you may find yourself relying on high-interest credit cards or loans to cover unexpected costs.

Building an emergency fund takes time and dedication, but it's worth the effort. It's an essential part of your financial plan and a key to financial security. Here's what you need to know to get started.

1. Set a Goal

Before you start saving, decide how much money you want to have in your emergency fund. It's generally recommended to save 3-6 months' worth of expenses in case of an emergency. This could mean anything from a job loss to a medical emergency.

Once you've set a goal, break it down into smaller, more achievable goals. For example, if your goal is to save $10,000 for an emergency fund, you might set a goal of saving $500 each month for the next 20 months.

2. Make a Budget

A budget is an essential tool for building an emergency fund. It will help you identify areas where you can cut back on spending and free up more cash for savings.

Start by tracking your spending for one month. This will give you an idea of where your money is going. Then, look for ways to reduce your spending. Can you give up cable and stream your favorite shows online? Can you save money on groceries by shopping at discount stores?

Once you've identified areas where you can cut back, create a budget that allocates your income to cover essential expenses, savings, and discretionary spending.

3. Open a Savings Account

Once you've identified areas to cut back and created a budget, it's time to open a savings account. Look for an account with a high interest rate and no or low fees.

You can also set up a direct deposit from your paycheck into the account. This will help you save more money and make it easier to meet your goals.

4. Automate Your Savings

Once you have a savings account, automate your savings. Set up a monthly transfer from your checking to your savings account. This way, you'll be able to save without having to think about it.

You can also set up automatic transfers for irregular expenses. For example, if you know you'll have to pay for car insurance every six months, you can set up an automatic transfer to cover the cost. This will help you stay on top of your bills and save more money.

5. Monitor Your Progress

Finally, make sure to monitor your progress. Track your spending and savings each month and adjust your budget as needed. This will help you stay on track and reach your goals faster.

Building an emergency fund is an important part of your financial plan. With dedication and the steps outlined above, you can create a fund that will give you financial security in times of need. Good luck!

Reasons to Have an Emergency Fund

Financial planning is an important part of life, regardless of your income level or where you're at in life. Everyone should have an emergency fund, and here are eight reasons why.

1. Unexpected Expenses

Unexpected expenses happen all the time, and they can be tough to deal with if you don't have an emergency fund. An emergency fund will help you cover the costs of these unexpected expenses, such as car repairs, medical bills, or home repairs. Having an emergency fund will give you peace of mind that you have money set aside in case something comes up.

2. Avoid High Interest Debt

If you don't have an emergency fund and an unexpected expense pops up, you may have to turn to high interest debt such as credit cards or payday loans. These types of debt can be very costly and can quickly spiral out of control if you're not careful. An emergency fund can help you avoid having to turn to high interest debt in an emergency situation.

3. Protect Your Credit Score

Having an emergency fund can help you protect your credit score by reducing your reliance on credit cards and other forms of high interest debt. If you don't have an emergency fund and you need to put an unexpected expense on a credit card, it can take a toll on your credit score. An emergency fund will help you avoid this situation.

4. Keeps You from Having to Borrow from Family or Friends

Having an emergency fund will help you avoid having to borrow money from family or friends in an emergency.

This can be an uncomfortable situation, and having an emergency fund will help you avoid it.

5. Peace of Mind

Having an emergency fund will give you peace of mind knowing that you have money set aside in case of an emergency. This can be a huge relief, and it can help you stay focused and productive in your day-to-day life.

6. Prepare for Potential Job Loss

No one likes to think about losing their job, but it's important to be prepared. An emergency fund can help you bridge the gap between jobs if you find yourself out of work.

7. Protect Retirement Savings

Retirement savings should not be used for short-term expenses, such as unexpected medical bills or car repairs. An emergency fund can help you cover these expenses without having to dip into your retirement savings.

8. Allows You to Take Advantage of Opportunities

Having an emergency fund can give you the freedom to take advantage of opportunities when they arise without having to worry about money. This could be anything from taking a class or buying a plane ticket to see family or taking a risk on a business opportunity.

Having an emergency fund is an important part of financial planning. An emergency fund can help you cover unexpected expenses, protect your credit score, keep you from having to borrow from family or friends, and more. Start building your emergency fund today so that you'll be prepared for whatever life throws your way.

How to Start an Emergency Fund

Starting an emergency fund can be a daunting task, especially for those who have not previously been in the habit of saving money. But having an emergency fund is essential for financial security, and can help you protect yourself from unexpected expenses and setbacks. With the right advice and planning, you can easily start and maintain an emergency fund to protect yourself and your family.

The first step in setting up an emergency fund is to determine how much money you want to put aside each month. It is generally recommended that you save at least 3-6 months worth of living expenses. This means that you should save enough money to cover rent/mortgage payments, utilities, food, transportation, and other necessary expenses for at least three months. You may choose to save more, but it is important to have at least this much saved in case of an emergency.

Once you have determined how much you need to save each month, you will need to open a separate account to save your money in. You may choose to open a savings account at a local bank or credit union, or you may opt for an online savings account. Whichever you choose, be sure that it offers a competitive interest rate and is FDIC-insured. This will ensure that your money is safe and grows over time.

Once you have opened your account, it is important to stay disciplined in your savings. Set up an automatic transfer from your checking account to your emergency fund account each month, and make sure the money is transferred before you are tempted to spend it. If you find yourself struggling to save, consider setting up a budget that helps you track your spending and allocate money to your emergency fund.

In addition to saving money, it is also important to protect your emergency fund from unforeseen risks. Consider purchasing insurance to protect your savings from theft, natural disasters, and other unexpected events. You may also want to consider investing in a high-yield savings account to help your money grow faster.

Finally, it is important to remember that your emergency fund is for emergencies only. Avoid the temptation to use your fund for non-essential expenses, as this could leave you without money in case of an unexpected expense.

Instead, focus on building your fund and protecting it from any unforeseen risks.

Starting an emergency fund is an important part of financial planning, and can help you protect yourself from unexpected expenses and setbacks. By following the steps outlined above, you can easily start and maintain an emergency fund to protect yourself and your family. With the right advice and planning, you can ensure that you are prepared for any unexpected events that may arise.

CHAPTER 5: Investing for Retirement

It's never too early to start planning for retirement. Retirement planning requires a great deal of thought and careful consideration, but with the right knowledge and resources, it can be both an enjoyable and rewarding experience. Retirement planning is all about taking a long-term approach to your financial security. This means investing in a wide variety of assets, including stocks, bonds, mutual funds, and other securities. The goal is to create a portfolio that is diversified and will have sufficient funds to provide for your retirement. Here's a look at some of the basics of retirement planning and financial planning for retirement.

1. Understand the Basics of Investing

The first step in retirement planning is to understand the basics of investing, including understanding different investment types, risk levels, and how to create a diversified portfolio. Investing in stocks and bonds is a great way to build wealth over time. When you invest, you're essentially putting your money to work and allowing it to compound over time. It's important to understand how different investments can provide different returns, so that you can create a diversified portfolio that will help you achieve your retirement goals.

2. Estimate Your Retirement Expenses

Before you begin investing for retirement, you need to have an idea of how much money you'll need to cover your expenses during retirement. This includes both fixed and variable expenses, such as housing, food, transportation, and medical expenses. You should also factor in any anticipated inflation, as well as any changes in your lifestyle. Once you have an estimate of your retirement expenses, you can begin to determine how much you need to save and invest to reach your retirement goals.

3. Choose Investment Accounts

Once you have an idea of your retirement expenses and goals, you can begin to choose the best investment accounts for your needs. There are a variety of retirement accounts, including traditional and Roth IRAs, 401(k)s, and annuities. Each of these accounts has its own advantages and disadvantages, so it's important to research each one to determine which one is right for you.

4. Invest Wisely

Once you've chosen your accounts, it's important to invest wisely. Investing in a variety of assets, such as stocks, bonds, and mutual funds, can help you create a diversified portfolio that can withstand market fluctuations. It's also important to understand how different investments can perform in different markets, so that you can make informed decisions about your investments.

5. Monitor Your Portfolio

Once you've established your portfolio, it's important to monitor it regularly to ensure that you're on track to reach your retirement goals. This means staying up to date on the performance of your investments, as well as making adjustments when necessary. As the markets fluctuate and your goals change, you should update your portfolio accordingly to ensure that it's performing at its best.

Retirement planning is an important part of financial planning, and it's never too early to start. With the right knowledge and resources, you can create a portfolio that will provide for your retirement needs and help you enjoy your golden years. Investing for retirement isn't a one-time event, but rather an ongoing process that requires careful planning and ongoing monitoring. By taking the time to understand the basics of investing and creating a diversified portfolio, you can ensure that you're taking the right steps towards achieving your retirement goals.

Retirement Accounts

Retirement accounts are one of the best ways to create a secure financial future for yourself. Retirement accounts are created to help individuals save for their retirement years, so they can live comfortably in their later years. In this article, we will discuss the basics of retirement accounts and how they can help you in financial planning.

First and foremost, it's important to understand what a retirement account is and how it works. A retirement account is an investment vehicle that allows you to set aside money for retirement. These accounts are managed by financial institutions, such as banks or brokerages, and are tax-advantaged. This means that you may be able to enjoy tax deductions when you contribute to your retirement account, as well as tax-deferred growth on the money that you save.

The most common types of retirement accounts are 401(k)s, IRAs, and Roth IRAs. A 401(k) is a workplace retirement plan that is sponsored by an employer. An IRA (Individual Retirement Account) is an account that can be opened by an individual to save for retirement. Roth IRAs are similar to traditional IRAs, but the money you contribute to a Roth IRA is taxed upfront and grows tax-free.

When it comes to financial planning, retirement accounts are an essential component. They are the foundation of a secure financial future, as they allow you to save money for the future. Retirement accounts also provide tax benefits, which can help to reduce your overall tax bill.

When beginning to plan for retirement, it's important to understand how much money you will need to save. This is especially true if you are relying solely on retirement accounts for your income in retirement. It's a good idea to consult a financial planner or retirement planner to get an estimate of how much you should save.

Once you have an estimate of how much you should save, you can start to look into which retirement accounts are right for you. As mentioned earlier, there are three main types of retirement accounts: 401(k)s, IRAs, and Roth IRAs. Each type of account comes with its own set of features and benefits. It's important to research each type of account and understand the features and benefits of each so that you can make an informed decision on which one is right for you.

When it comes to retirement accounts, it's also important to understand the different types of investments you can make. You can choose to invest in stocks, bonds, mutual funds, and other investments. Each type of investment has its own set of risks and rewards, so it's important to understand how each type works and decide which type is best for your retirement needs.

Finally, it's important to understand the rules and regulations associated with retirement accounts. Each type of account has its own set of rules and regulations that you must abide by in order to maintain the tax-advantaged status of the account. It's important to understand these rules and regulations and follow them to ensure that you are able to maximize the benefits of your retirement accounts.

Retirement accounts are an essential component of any financial plan. They provide tax benefits, allow you to save for the future, and provide you with the opportunity to invest in a variety of investments. It's important to understand the basics of retirement accounts and how they can help you in financial planning. With the right knowledge, you can create a secure financial future for yourself.

Investing Strategies

Investing strategies are an important part of financial planning. Whether you are just starting out or are already an experienced investor, having a sound plan in place can help you set and reach your financial goals.

At the very basic level, investing is about putting your money to work for you. It is about taking the money you have today and using it to generate more money in the future. Whether you are saving for retirement, a college education, or other long-term goals, investing can help you reach those goals faster.

Before investing your hard-earned money, it's important to understand the basics. Here are some of the most common and important investing strategies to consider when creating your financial plan:

1. Set a Goal

The first step in any financial plan is to set a goal. That goal should be specific and measurable, such as having $500,000 saved by the time you turn 65, or having enough money to pay for your child's college education in 10 years. Setting a goal will help you determine the amount of money you need to save and invest each month, and what type of investments are best suited for your situation.

2. Determine Your Risk Tolerance

Your risk tolerance is an important factor when it comes to investing. It is the amount of risk you are comfortable taking with your money. Generally, the more risk you are willing to take on, the greater the potential for reward. However, it is important to understand that there is also greater potential for loss.

3. Create a Diversified Portfolio

Creating a diversified portfolio is one of the most important investing strategies. This means investing in a variety of different types of investments, such as stocks, bonds, mutual funds, and ETFs. This will help you spread out the risk and maximize your returns.

43

4. Rebalance Regularly

Rebalancing your portfolio on a regular basis is an essential part of financial planning. This means that when certain investments in your portfolio become more or less valuable than others, you will need to sell some of the more valuable investments and purchase more of the less valuable ones, in order to keep the balance of your portfolio in line with your goals.

5. Utilize Tax-Advantaged Accounts

There are several types of tax-advantaged accounts, such as 401(k)s, IRAs, and 529 plans, that can help you save for retirement or other long-term goals. These accounts allow you to save and invest money on a tax-deferred basis, meaning that you don't have to pay taxes on the money until you take it out. This can help you maximize the growth of your investments.

6. Take Advantage of Automation

Automation is a great way to make sure you stay on track with your investing goals. Automated investing services, such as robo-advisors, can help you create a diversified portfolio and manage it on your behalf. This can be especially helpful if you don't have the time or experience to manage your investments yourself.

7. Have a Plan for Market Volatility

Investing in the stock market involves taking on some risk, and it is important to understand that markets can be volatile. Having a plan in place for when the markets do move can help you stay on track with your goals. For example, you may want to set a certain level of losses that would trigger you to sell certain investments. This can help you minimize losses and protect your portfolio from major losses.

These are just a few of the investing strategies that you should consider when creating your financial plan. Ultimately, the most important thing is to take the time to understand the different types of investments available and how they can help you reach your financial goals. With a sound investment strategy in place, you can take control of your financial future and reach your goals.

CHAPTER 6: Insurance Planning

When it comes to financial planning, insurance planning is an essential part of the process. Insurance planning is the process of determining the types and amounts of insurance needed to protect you and your family from financial losses due to illness, death, or other unexpected events. Financial planning is an important part of planning for the future, and insurance planning is an integral part of the process.

When you think about insurance planning, the first thing you may think about is life insurance. Life insurance is an important part of the financial planning process because it can provide a death benefit to your family in the event of your death. This death benefit can be used to pay off debts, provide an income for your family, and help to cover funeral expenses. There are several different types of life insurance policies available, including term life insurance, whole life insurance, and universal life insurance. Each type of policy has its own advantages and disadvantages, so it is important to discuss your options with a qualified financial planner to choose the right policy for you.

Another type of insurance that should be considered in the financial planning process is disability insurance. Disability insurance provides income protection if you become disabled and cannot work. Depending on the type of policy you choose, it can provide a partial or full income replacement so you can continue to pay your bills and maintain your lifestyle.

Long-term care insurance is another important part of the financial planning process. This type of insurance pays for medical and non-medical services for those who are unable to take care of themselves due to age, disability, or illness. This type of insurance can help to cover the costs of in-home care, assisted living, and nursing home care.

Property and casualty insurance is also an important part of the financial planning process. This type of insurance provides coverage for damage or loss to your property due to a variety of events, including fire, theft, and natural disasters. This type of insurance can also provide coverage for liability if someone is injured on your property.

Finally, umbrella insurance is an important part of financial planning as well. This type of insurance provides an extra layer of coverage on top of your other policies. It can provide additional liability coverage in the event of a major lawsuit or other legal action.

Insurance planning is an important part of the financial planning process, and it is important to consider all of your options when making decisions about the types and amounts of insurance you need. It is important to discuss your insurance needs with a qualified financial planner so that you can make the best decision for your financial future.

Types of Insurance

Insurance is an important part of financial planning, but it can be a confusing topic. There are many different types of insurance, and each type serves a different purpose. It's important to understand the different types of insurance so that you can make informed decisions when it comes to protecting yourself, your loved ones, and your assets.

Life Insurance

Life insurance is a type of insurance that pays out a lump sum of money to your beneficiaries upon your death. It is designed to help your loved ones financially after you are gone. There are two main types of life insurance – term life insurance and whole life insurance.

Term life insurance is a type of life insurance that pays out a lump sum of money to your beneficiaries upon your death. It provides coverage for a specific period of time, typically 10, 20, or 30 years. It is typically inexpensive and is the most common type of life insurance.

Whole life insurance is a type of life insurance that pays out a lump sum of money to your beneficiaries upon your death. It provides coverage for your entire life, as long as you continue to pay the premiums. Whole life insurance is typically more expensive than term life insurance, but it also has a cash value component that can be used as an investment.

Health Insurance

Health insurance is a type of insurance that helps cover medical expenses. It can help you pay for doctor's visits, hospital stays, prescription drugs, and other medical services. There are two main types of health insurance – employer-sponsored health insurance and individual health insurance.

Employer-sponsored health insurance is a type of health insurance that is provided by an employer. It typically covers the employee and their dependents and is paid for by the employer.

Individual health insurance is a type of health insurance that is purchased by an individual. It is typically more expensive than employer-sponsored health insurance, but it can provide more comprehensive coverage.

Auto Insurance

Auto insurance is a type of insurance that helps cover the costs of vehicle repairs and medical expenses in the event of an accident. It can also provide coverage for other expenses such as towing and rental car expenses. There are two main types of auto insurance – liability insurance and comprehensive coverage.

Liability insurance is a type of auto insurance that provides coverage for damage to another person's vehicle or property. It does not provide coverage for damage to your vehicle.

Comprehensive coverage is a type of auto insurance that provides coverage for damage to your vehicle. It can also provide coverage for theft, vandalism, and other types of losses.

Homeowners Insurance

Homeowners insurance is a type of insurance that helps cover the costs of repairing or replacing your home in the event of a disaster. It can also provide coverage for personal belongings, such as furniture and clothing, in the event of a disaster. There are two main types of homeowners insurance – dwelling coverage and personal liability coverage.

Dwelling coverage is a type of homeowners insurance that provides coverage for damage to your home. It does not provide coverage for personal belongings.

Personal liability coverage is a type of homeowners insurance that provides coverage for liability claims. It can help cover medical bills and other costs if someone is injured on your property.

Renters Insurance

Renters insurance is a type of insurance that helps cover the costs of repairing or replacing your personal belongings in the event of a disaster. It can also provide coverage for liability claims if someone is injured on the property.

Umbrella Insurance

Umbrella insurance is a type of insurance that provides additional coverage above and beyond your other insurance policies. It can help protect you from costly lawsuits and other liabilities.

By understanding the different types of insurance and the coverage they provide, you can make informed decisions about which types of insurance are best for your situation. Insurance is an important part of financial planning, and it is important to make sure that you have the right coverage in place to protect yourself, your loved ones, and your assets.

Risk Management Strategies

Risk management is an essential part of financial planning. As a financial planner, you must be able to assess, identify, and manage the risks associated with a range of financial decisions. Risk management strategies are designed to help protect your investments and ensure your financial future.

When looking at risk management strategies, there are two main types: active and passive. Active risk management strategies involve actively managing your investments to achieve a desired risk-return balance. This could include diversifying investments, hedging, and using derivatives. Passive risk management strategies involve taking a more hands-off approach and relying on the markets to provide the desired return. This could include investing in index funds and ETFs.

No matter which strategies you choose, it's important to understand the risks associated with each type of investment. This includes understanding the potential rewards and risks, as well as the costs associated with each type of investment. It's also important to understand the importance of diversification, as this can help spread out risk and reduce the potential for large losses.

When assessing the risks associated with a particular investment, it's important to consider the following factors:

-The volatility of the investment. This is the degree to which the value of the investment will fluctuate over time. Generally, the more volatile an investment is, the higher the potential for losses.

-The liquidity of the investment. This is the ease with which the investment can be converted into cash. Generally, the more liquid an investment is, the easier it is to cash out when needed.

-The cost of the investment. This is the total amount of money you'll need to invest in order to purchase the investment. Generally, the higher the cost, the more money you'll need to invest.

-The risk associated with the investment. This is the likelihood that the investment will lose value. Generally, the higher the risk, the greater the potential for losses.

Once you've assessed the risks associated with a particular investment, you can then decide which risk management strategies are best for you. Generally, the goal is to reduce the risk of loss while still maintaining a reasonable return on your investment. Some strategies you might consider include diversifying your investments, using hedging strategies, and using derivatives.

Diversifying your investments is one of the most effective ways to reduce risk. By investing in a variety of asset classes, you can spread out the risk associated with any one investment. This can help reduce the potential for large losses if one particular investment fails.

Hedging strategies involve using derivatives to reduce the risk associated with a particular investment. For example, you might use a futures contract to hedge against the risk of a stock price decreasing. Similarly, an option contract can be used to hedge against the risk of a stock price increasing.

Finally, derivatives can also be used to increase the potential return of an investment. For example, you might use a futures contract to take advantage of movements in the price of a commodity. Similarly, an option contract might be used to take advantage of movements in the price of a stock.

No matter which risk management strategies you choose, it's important to understand the risks associated with each type of investment. This includes understanding the potential rewards and risks, as well as the costs associated with each type of investment. By understanding these risks, you can create a more effective financial plan and ensure your financial future.

CHAPTER 7: Estate Planning

Estate planning is an important part of financial planning. It involves making arrangements for the transfer of your assets, such as property, investments, and funds, to your beneficiaries upon your death. It also involves protecting those assets from taxes and other liabilities. In this article, we'll discuss the basics of estate planning and how it can help you ensure that your family is taken care of after you're gone.

First of all, you need to understand what estate planning is. Estate planning is the process of creating a plan for transferring your assets to your designated beneficiaries upon your death. This involves creating a will, setting up trusts, establishing a durable power of attorney, and creating other legal documents. It also involves making arrangements for the payment of taxes, debts, and other liabilities.

When it comes to estate planning, it's important to understand the tax implications of transferring your assets. Depending on where you live, you may be subject to different tax laws. For example, some states impose an inheritance tax on assets transferred to certain beneficiaries. It's important to understand these laws and make sure that you're in compliance with them.

Another important consideration when it comes to estate planning is the type of assets you want to transfer. Depending on how you set up your estate, you may be able to transfer assets to beneficiaries free of taxes. You may also be able to set up trusts or other legal entities to protect your assets from creditors, or to ensure that they are distributed to your beneficiaries in a way that is beneficial to them.

When it comes to estate planning, it's also important to make sure that your beneficiaries are taken care of after you're gone. This can include making arrangements for their financial security, such as life insurance policies, setting up trusts for their care, and providing for their education. It's also important to make sure that your wishes are carried out when it comes to your assets, including how they should be distributed and who should receive them.

Estate planning can be a complicated process, but it's important to ensure that your family is taken care of after you're gone. It's also important to understand the tax implications of transferring your assets, and to make sure that you're in compliance with the laws of your state. With the right planning, you can ensure that your family is taken care of after you're gone.

Writing a Will

Writing a will is an important step in financial planning. It ensures that your assets and property are distributed according to your wishes after you die. Without a will, your estate will be subject to the laws of your state, which may not reflect your wishes or intentions.

When writing a will, there are several important things to consider. First, you will need to decide who will act as your executor. This person is responsible for managing your estate after your death. They will be in charge of making sure your assets are distributed according to your will. It is important that you choose someone who is reliable and trustworthy.

You will also need to decide who will receive your assets. You can specify any person, organization, or charity as a beneficiary. You can also name alternate beneficiaries in case your primary beneficiaries die before you.

In addition to deciding who gets what, you will need to decide how your assets will be distributed. For example, you can specify that your assets be divided equally among your beneficiaries. You can also specify that certain assets be given to a specific beneficiary.

Finally, you will need to make arrangements for the care of any minor children you may have. You can appoint a guardian to care for them if both parents die before they reach the age of majority. It is also wise to set up a trust fund for them, so that their money is managed properly and not spent before they are old enough to manage it themselves.

Writing a will is an important part of financial planning. It ensures that your wishes are carried out after you die. It is important to consult with an experienced attorney to ensure that your will is properly drafted and that all of the necessary provisions are included. With proper planning, you can ensure that your assets are distributed according to your wishes.

Beneficiary Designations

When it comes to financial planning, many people often don't think about beneficiary designations. However, beneficiary designations are a crucial part of financial planning, as they determine who will receive your assets upon your death. Knowing how to properly designate beneficiaries is a key element of any good financial plan.

A beneficiary designation is a document that names the people or organizations that you want to receive assets in the event of your death. These assets can include life insurance policies, individual retirement accounts (IRAs), 401(k)s, annuities, and bank accounts.

When creating a beneficiary designation, you should make sure that the document accurately reflects your wishes. The most important aspect of a beneficiary designation is to make sure that all of your assets are accounted for and that you have named the correct individuals or organizations that should receive your assets.

It is also important to keep your beneficiary designations up to date. As life circumstances change, so should your beneficiaries. For example, if you get married or divorced, you will need to update your beneficiaries to ensure that the right person receives your assets.

It is also important to consider the tax implications of beneficiary designations. Depending on your situation, certain assets may be subject to income or estate taxes. It is important to consult with a financial or tax advisor to make sure that your beneficiary designations are in compliance with the law.

Beneficiary designations are an integral part of any financial plan. Taking the time to make sure that your beneficiary designations are accurate and up to date is an important way to ensure that your assets are distributed the way that you want them to be. It is important to consult

with a financial professional to make sure that your
financial plan is in order.

CHAPTER 8: Conclusion

Financial planning is an important skill that everyone should learn. It can help you achieve financial security, build wealth, and make sure your money is working for you. Financial planning is the process of managing your finances to achieve personal economic satisfaction. It is a lifelong process that involves setting goals, analyzing your current financial situation, identifying potential risks and opportunities, creating a plan to achieve your goals, and implementing and monitoring the plan.

Financial planning is the foundation of a secure financial future. It helps you make smart choices about how to use your money and manage debt in order to reach your goals. Financial planning can help you save for retirement, pay for college, buy a house, and build a rainy day fund. It can also help you reduce taxes, maximize investments, and protect your assets.

The first step in financial planning is to set realistic financial goals. Decide what you want to accomplish with your money and develop a plan to reach those goals. Consider your short-term and long-term goals, such as saving for a house or retirement, creating an emergency fund, or paying off debt.

The next step is to assess your current financial situation. Take an inventory of your assets, liabilities, income, and expenses. Make sure you understand your current financial position and have an accurate view of your net worth.

Once you have an understanding of your current financial situation, you can begin to identify potential risks and opportunities. Consider potential risks such as inflation, market volatility, and unexpected expenses. Identify opportunities such as tax savings, investment returns, and additional income sources.

The third step in financial planning is to create a plan to achieve your goals. Make sure you have a budget that reflects your current financial situation and goals. Develop a plan to pay off debt, save for retirement, and invest for the future. Develop strategies to protect your assets and reduce taxes.

Once you have developed a plan, the fourth step is to implement and monitor it. Make sure you stick to your budget and follow through on your financial plan. Monitor your investments and track your progress towards achieving your goals.

Financial planning is a process that requires dedication and discipline. It is an important skill that everyone should learn in order to secure their financial future. Financial planning can help you make smart choices about how to manage your money and reach your financial goals. With a little time and effort, you can create a plan to reach your financial goals and secure your future.